GENTLENESS

in John of the Cross

THOMAS KANE

SLG PRESS
Convent of the Incarnation
Fairacres Oxford

ISBN 0 7283 0105 9
ISSN 0307-1405

This article, originally published in *Contemplative Review* in 1982,
is reprinted here with the permission of
The Association of Contemplative Sisters.

Printed and bound by Will Print, Oxford, England.

Gentleness in John of the Cross

THE TITLE for this article may come as a surprise to some. Those who do not know John of the Cross well often have the impression that he is very harsh. Nothing but *nada, nada, nada* (which is Spanish for 'nothing'). This seems to correspond with the image some of his contemporaries had of him. Some feared he would be severe and rigorously intransigent as a confessor and so avoided him. But one woman who felt that way and found herself in his confessional anyway was surprised when he told her that a holy confessor should not frighten people. 'I' he said, 'am not so, but the holier the confessor, the gentler he is and the less he is scandalized at other people's faults, because he understands man's weak condition better'.[1] Years later she told of the gentle way in which he dealt with her and helped her change her life.

In a parallel way, friars who knew him only by reputation were afraid to go and live with him because they thought they would find in him a harsh and uncompromising superior who would make them enter by force the path of the most rigid penances. This was changed very quickly by their living with him. Fr Crisogono in his *Life* of the saint several times uses the word 'gentle' to characterize the way John, as Prior, led his communities and corrected their faults.[2] He often took them out for days on the hillsides to bask in the beauties of nature, and was known for his careful and affectionate personal care for the sick. He seems to have had a gift for telling amusing stories to cheer up his brothers who so enjoyed his presence that they did not like it when he had to miss community recreation.[3] After describing a whole series of examples of John's gentle and deeply affectionate interest in and care for the members of his

1

communities, Fr Crisogono suggests that this makes it easy to understand 'the deep and tender affection which all his subjects gave him'.[4]

As we become increasingly familiar with the writings of John of the Cross the same transformation should happen: a first reading of *The Ascent of Mount Carmel* might impress us with its depth and rigour; but as we gradually come to know his mind through repeated and sympathetic reading, this quality of gentleness comes more and more to the fore. We begin to see why he says things like 'O sweet cautery' or 'O happy night'; and why he says that only a heart made gentle can experience the Word dwelling gently in its depth.[5] Indeed, we come to see that this movement towards gentleness is central to John's vision of how God draws us into himself.

The Roots of Violence and Gentleness

John is convinced that the human heart was made for union, human and divine; more than that, he knows it from experience. Anything less violates it. Jesus is the radiant symbol of this, and the One in whom the Father brings it about. He is our true destiny; and our hearts suffer violence until they are transformed in and into the heart of Jesus; that is, until in Jesus we experience the Father's love for us and are united with one another in intimate fidelity. For John, it is always the Holy Spirit who draws us into Jesus' heart and so into the inner life of the Trinity, to imitate Jesus by living on the will of the Father.[6] This means that we become fully human only as we become God, by sharing in his life.[7]

This is our destiny; but it is not where we begin. We begin shattered by the awful fear that we are all alone, bound by the suspicion that we are unlovable. For John these ingrained tendencies are the result of original sin, for this rebellion has broken the union that should obtain between God and man, man and man, and within man himself. Further, these destructive orientations are often reinforced by our painful day-to-day personal experiences. Ravaged by these, we set out to protect the self, a self that seems isolated, that we fear is somehow unlovable, a false self, a violated self. To this fractured self the obvious way

2

to safety is to seize control, put up defences, always seek pleasure, use others, avoid pain. The violated self sets out to save itself by ruthless means. This only does further violence to the self and leads to violence against others. But this it cannot see, cannot afford to see.[8]

This is in marked contrast to what we see in Jesus as he is portrayed for us in the gospels. For example, in Luke 23:35-46 Jesus, as he hangs on the cross, is goaded repeatedly to 'save himself'. When his human weakness is exposed to all, his oppressors egg him on to be jealous of God. In his agony they tease him with the idea of doing what they covertly try to do themselves: play God. It is the great and fundamental evil that wells up out of the violated self; it is the Garden of Eden replayed: the wish to be God and save one's self. It is the diabolical arrogance that distorts the unity of all reality. The paradox is that Jesus, the God-man, refuses to do precisely this. Instead he chooses to be what man needs to be. In prayer, in absolute trust, he hands himself and his life over to his Father. He dies praying 'Father, into your hands I commend my spirit'.[9]

Jesus, then, chooses to be the Father's little one, united to him and relying on him alone. Violence may bring Jesus to this awful death; but his death overcomes this very violence. Indeed, he opens up for the rest of us a whole new way of living. This is what Luke means to bring out in the story of the good thief. In Jesus our hearts can now find what they desperately needed; union with the Father, communion with each other. Jesus' obedience unto death has broken the hold that rebellion has held over all creation. The deep union for which we were made can once again be ours; and the more we begin to experience this in our lives the more we are freed to leave behind the false self that we have created as a defence and to let the true self, the Christ-self, to be created in us. Very simply, isolation violates our deepest need: to be loved and loving; whereas communion heals us, opening up to us the way of gentleness.

John's Way from Violence to Gentleness

This is exactly what John tells us. When you pick up the *Ascent-Night* (*The Ascent of Mount Carmel* and its companion volume, *The Dark Night of the Soul*) you have before you John's understanding of how God leads us to the gentleness of *The Living Flame of Love*, where we are so simplified that the violence of separation is banished.[10] We are gentle enough to experience the awesome gentleness of the inner life of God;[11] and to see all of creation as it really is, in God, and love it with the over-whelming but gentle love with which God loves it.[12] Still, if the end is simplicity, the way is often difficult. The transformation of a false self, that thinks it needs to be God, into a self that knows it is loved, and so can choose to be just man, may be a movement from violence to gentleness but it is often wrenching.

If we read the *Ascent-Night* straight through we will find a presentation of this way in a logical order. For John, human nature is undivided, whole: part sensible, part spiritual. Our sensible nature must be freed of its instinctive orientation to seize on something, anything, to make us feel real. The end result of this purification is to attune man's sensible nature to his spirit. But this is only a preparation for the crucial struggle. Man, now united in himself, must be transformed, for the violence that has distorted man is rooted in the spirit. This double healing is further divided into two phases: what man led by the Spirit must do, and what remains totally beyond him, and so what he must wait for God to do. This is John's logical framework and more or less sets up the structure of the *Ascent-Night*.[13] The *Ascent* deals with the active phase: night of sense in Book I and night of spirit in Books II and III. The *Dark Night* deals with the passive phases: night of sense in Book I, night of spirit in Book II.

A careful reading, of both the *Ascent-Night* texts[14] and of one's own experience and that of others, reveals that people usually do not develop according to this logical order. Let me briefly sketch what often does happen, and then come back to describe in a little more detail what some of this looks like.

In the *Ascent* I, John tells us that our disordered appetites do us violence. They weary, torment, defile and weaken us.[15]

4

They promise but cannot give us the deep union we need; indeed, they lead us further away from it. In this dilemma the Spirit touches us, attracting us to Jesus. We begin to see that he moves in a world of incredible depth and integrity; but most of all we see in him the invitation of his loving Father calling us home. This has an incalculable appeal to our true but scarcely discovered selves. To be grasped by this vision of Jesus is to begin to be healed. Here, Jesus is the one who calls us, who inspires us with his hope for us and mankind; and like the disciples in Mark 1:16-20 we follow him. We do not understand him well. We are not really sure what it is that he promises; but somehow we know that this is what our hearts have always looked for, often in the wrong place. To know Jesus better we begin to meditate on the gospels; and as this becomes part of us we grow to love him more deeply. Through the medium of this love, we come to understand him better and to want to live as he did.

And what was at the core of Jesus' life? John tells us it was to do the will of the Father.[16] As we set out to follow Jesus in this we discover how free he was and how burdened we are. He was poor; he chose to serve; he didn't worry about much that concerns us. To be free enough to go with him we gradually, judiciously, resolutely begin to let go of the things we have become accustomed to live off, and which have come to own us. This spells itself out in the aridity, frustration and boredom associated with the active night of sense; and yet a deeper love draws us into this night and sustains us in it.[17] At least at times we have a real sense of the Beloved's presence in meditation, or at Mass, and our hearts are strengthened to follow him.

There comes a time though when God moves in a new way, and the things to which we cling are taken from us.[18] This is the passive night of sense; and John concentrates his analysis on our interior sense, imagination.[19] This is the point where sense and spirit meet in us, for understanding is insight into the data presented by the imagination. We have used this understanding in meditation; and now it is gone. We sit down to meditate and draw a blank; the imagination doesn't flow. With this the sense of the Beloved's presence that has been so crucial in our lives is withdrawn. This leads us on to the active night of the spirit and to a further choice. It is a question of trust. Will we, now, choose to open ourselves and wait for a God who is un-imaginable, in-conceivable?[20] Will we let the sensible experience of his presence go? If we do, then there is a pure inflow of God into our depths beyond anything we can experience, or understand.

If we can say 'yes' here, if day in and day out we can let this mysterious 'yes' sink into us, then a huge unification and simplification of the whole person takes place. The first three nights mingle together and bring us to the point where the events of our lives more and more provide us with the opportunity to trust in God alone. Usually it is only after years of this deeply faithful and fruitful living that a soul is brought into the final cleansing of the passive night of the spirit, where the very roots of our inclinations towards self-salvation, terror and guilt, are stripped from us. Made totally simple, when everything we could cling to is gone (either given up or taken away) then there is only God. This is the moment of the great awakening of the *Living Flame*.

Can we call this terrible stripping gentle? Even if it moves us from a violently self-destructive way of living to a gentle one, isn't the way itself something that does terrible violence to us? John does not think so, even though he calls the way a crucifixion.[21] In the *Dark Night* II, 9, 10 he asks specifically why this inflow of God into the human heart is so painful, and in the next paragraph he gives his answer very succinctly. It is only because we are distorted and weakened that this experience of God's healing presence is at times terrible.[22]

In the *Ascent* II, 17, 3 he adds another piece to the picture. This movement of healing is in stages adapted to the needs and development of each individual. It is ordered, gradual and gentle even as it is relentless and taxing to the limit. This is parallel to what St Ignatius Loyola says in his introductory observations on the *Spiritual Exercises*: the person giving the *Exercises* is to adapt himself or herself to those whom he directs, understanding where they are and moving from there. Why? Because this is what God does. He accepts us as we are, with the structure of our personality, our strengths and weaknesses; and begins to heal us in a way that is geared to us.[23]

Further, because this is such a drastic healing, a reorientation towards our true destiny, our depths begin to come alive even in the midst of turmoil. The healing must be drastic, but it is also gentle. In the *Ascent* II, 7 where John is discussing the active night of spirit, the central theme of embracing the Cross of Christ in all things is presented and an unexpected question is asked: How does one know that it is the Cross of Christ one bears? John quotes Matthew 11:30, 'My yoke is sweet and my burden [the Cross] light'; we know we are bearing the Cross of Christ because deep down we are at peace. Why? Because we are being healed, not violated, at the very core of our being.

The life-giving character of this healing comes out also in John's repeated reinterpretation of the line in the first stanza of the poem 'The Dark Night': 'fired with love's urgent longings'. In the active night of sense of the *Ascent* I this line is interpreted as referring to the sensible attraction to, and presence of, Jesus that frees us to let go of other addictive forms of gratification.[24] In the passive night of sense of the *Dark Night* I it is the growing longing for God that transcends this sensible experience of his presence.[25] (The *Ascent* II and III which cover the active night of spirit are theoretically a commentary on the second stanza of the same poem although it is not discussed directly.) Then in the *Dark Night* II he returns a third time to this crucial line. Here he interprets it in terms of a passion of love. In the stripping that is the passive night of the spirit, a love of God that begins to take over the whole personality is being infused into the depths of the human heart.[26] It will reveal its true depth in the experience of union as the living flame that is the Holy Spirit.[27]

Perhaps I could say this again in a parable. One day, as a woman was walking down a street she saw a man sitting on a front porch, stroking a cat. She was so struck by the gentleness with which he did this that she crossed the street to get a better look. As she drew closer she was surprised to see that the cat's eyes glared, his back was arched, his fur stood on end and his claws dug into the floor of the porch. The man was very gently stroking the cat against the grain; and as he did so he was talking to the cat. Now, quite confused, she drew even nearer until she could hear what the man was saying as he stroked the cat so gently, though against the grain. 'Turn around cat.'

A Crucial Turning Point on the Way

Having sketched the basic structure of this movement towards gentleness, let's go back and see some of what it looks like in a little more detail. In particular, I am interested in how the passive night of sense and the active night of spirit flow into each other and gradually lead to a unification and simplification of the person that can be characterized as a 'gentling'. The first question to ask is what do people look like at this stage, that is, on the brink of the passive night of sense? They see themselves as faith-full, for they believe in Jesus, cling to him, and loyally follow in his way, as they see it. They meditate daily; are faithful to Mass and sacraments. They work hard at their vocation in life and are beginning to free themselves from attachments to sense gratification so that they can be like Jesus in all things. They can be very fervent; but they also have many imperfections.

They can be seduced by the progress they think they have made. This can express itself as a proneness to spiritual arrogance, a presumption that they are truly wise and in a position to criticize others. They can become grumblers. For example, there are conversations about what a religious order, or a parish, should obviously be, or obviously do, in which the spirit of the conversation is so arrogant, so proud, that it precludes almost any real discussion or any discernment of what God might really be doing.[28] Parallel to this is the temptation to parade oneself as holy, so that we live off the attention this gives us; and this while there is a harshness or a lack of simplicity in our hearts.[29] God becomes someone in our back pocket, instead of the ever mysterious Beloved who constantly calls us out of ourselves. We get attached to finding God in prayer; and when we don't experience his presence we get cranky and angry.[30] Or we get discouraged. We feel that others don't understand us;[31] they don't really see our goodness and wisdom and this puts us out of sorts. At other times it is our own failures that bring us crashing down. Having enjoyed too exalted an opinion of ourselves, we now are deflated and are ready to give up.[32] We begin to doubt that God really cares for us—even after all we have done for him.

The basic problem is that we are still very self-centred. We go to prayer more for the consolation we receive than for love of him who consoles us. We are just as possessive in our friendships and other relationships. Even our speech betrays us. We talk of: my friend, my class, my parish, my family or community; and that is exactly what we mean. We take what is the Lord's and make it our own.[33] Often there is still a great deal of habitual anger in us and any disappointment or frustration can bring it to the surface. We can become spiritual busybodies, quite caught up in the 'how come' syndrome.[34] 'How come I'm the only one at morning prayer, if we are supposed to be a praying community?' 'How come the office wants me to deal with this, if they won't?' 'How come I have to do this when . . . ?'

So we have basically good, loyal, prayerful people with a lot of rough edges. They get bored and feel sorry for themselves. They overestimate their surrender to God and underestimate their sinfulness. They can be arrogant one minute and discouraged the next. They mistake their impatience for zeal, their arrogance for candor. We see here a complex combination of sadness, resentment, confusion, guilt and a proneness to get fed up and feel sorry for one's self; in a word *acedia*, or spiritual sloth.[35]

When the time is right, God moves to change all of this by drawing the person into the passive night of sense. In the *Dark Night* I John's primary emphasis is on how this alters the way we pray. What happens is that we find we can no longer meditate. This sensible way of praying with its consolations is taken away from us. This determines the central structure of the book. In Chapter 8 he tells us what happens. In Chapter 9 he gives us the signs to discern the source of this inability: does it come from God or from sin and *acedia*? Chapter 10 tells us what we are to do; and Chapter 11 starts to speak of the effects of this night.

Now, the careful reader will notice that this material in the *Dark Night* is parallel to Chapters 12-15 of the *Ascent* II. This forces the question: what is the relation between the active night of spirit, which is the concern of the *Ascent* II and III, and the passive night of sense which we dealing with here in the *Dark Night* I? It seems that God creates a new situation in the soul, something which happens to the person, so it is passive. And this new situation confronts the person with a new choice. Will he choose to let go of the old way of finding God and wait for him when he can no longer understand or experience his presence? Here the emphasis is on the choice of the person, and so it is active. This is a pattern we will see again. The passive night of sense of the *Dark Night* I sets up and calls forth the active night of spirit of the *Ascent* II and III.

As before when we entered the active night of sense, an emptiness opens up before us. When you could meditate there was, at least at times, a tangible sense of God's presence; and besides you knew you were praying. Now things become so vague. You sit down to pray; you read the gospel story and this bland quiet comes upon you. It seems to be what you are drawn into, but is there anyone there? Is this just day-dreaming? At first it is very hard to tell. John tells us that there is a pure and gentle inflow of God into the soul; but because it happens on a level deeper than the conscious operations of the mind, it is also dark. And because the soul is not yet pure and gentle enough, it is not aware of this communion. It has to be made gentle. However, to let that happen it must choose to open itself up to this bland quiet. It must choose to wait for God in a way it can not experience or understand. So the passive night sets up a new choice. In this way the passive night of sense calls forth and flows into the active night of spirit.

As I have said, in the *Dark Night* I and the *Ascent* II John concentrates on how this alters our prayer. But it has profound consequences for the rest of our lives as well, detaching us from what we can experience and understand and teaching us to trust in God alone. Let me describe what some of this might look like. The kind of person we are trying to understand, at this stage in his or her development, usually has made a series of life-orientating commitments: to a religious community, or to a spouse, with a given life work or works, and many varied responsibilities. Often God uses the daily routines and obligations that flow from these commitments to transform us. There can come a day, for example, when the repetitive sameness of our lives begins to move in on us, offering us an unsought opportunity to face ourselves honestly. We tend to live in the future when there is the prospect of something new and exciting to do, when we can always think 'tomorrow I'll . . .' The boundless hopes and desires of our hearts, which are often selfish and sometimes sheer illusion, look to the future and keep us going. A whole life lived like this can let us hide from our real situation in the present. But confrontation with the endless daily sameness leaves no escape. We have to face the present; we have to look at the realities of our lives: prayer, fear, death, hope, conversion.

Now, if the basic life-orientating decisions we have made were good ones, then, probably the lives they have structured for us are basically gentle. The rhythms of silence and human sharing, prayer and work, fit us. They correspond to our hearts. Gently they bring us to God, to others and our true selves. Still, there is a persistence, a relentlessness to this that can be taxing, that allows no escape; and so there is pressure. While our minds and hearts gladly embraced this life, we are now brought starkly to the realization that there is more to it than this. There is a part of us that finds itself pressured, cramped, denied; and it looks desperately for an escape. We are not yet pure of heart and the privation which this daily sameness brings pushes to the surface the possessiveness, anger, fears and doubts that have been covered over. There is, at times, a ferocious desire to search for something else or a flight from what is given, and repetitively given.

Gently but relentlessly the mixed motives of our hearts are drawn out. Gradually we also begin to be aware that we could not face this on our own; nor do we have to, for God is moving in on us as we sit and wait for him in the bland silence of prayer. Both God and our day-to-day lives have a grip on us; and together they are changing us in ways we could not do for ourselves. We could stop them; but we don't. Somehow, though we might have trouble saying how or when, we have said 'yes' to both; and so we continue to be changed. Once again what happens to us and what we choose flow together.

These two movements of our lives keep working on us. The daily rhythm that gently but relentlessly squeezes us keeps bringing to the surface one central fact: we are not simple. This is expressed in our fears, our avoidance, at times, of silence, the restlessness that claws at us. Conjoined with this is the silent seeping of God into our hearts that keeps eroding the duplicity that is woven so deeply into us. Together they prepare us to face both the symptoms as they are forced to the surface and the root cause that lurks below. At first, even when we are most honest, we can see some of the symptoms but have only the vaguest sense of the root; but gradually, irrevocably, this too comes into focus. We begin to see that we have only partly accepted God's gift of his love to us. Part of us will have none of it.[36] Instead of his love, we want to control our own destiny. We harden our hearts.[37] We do not yet trust him enough to hand over to him the complete control of our lives. So, we resist him, clinging to our own attempts to control. Still, we have to be 'good people' so we exercise this control in acceptable ways. We are detached, prayerful, dedicated, loyal—more so than many; and this gives us a sense of our own integrity, indeed, superiority. Deep down we expect that in this way we can save ourselves. Others, and especially God, will *have* to give us what we want.

This has been there for years, and now in the events of our lives and in the silence of our prayer we become aware that Jesus is turning to us once again to say 'What do you want?'[38] and our lives make clear that it is not just to be his beloved and to love others no matter the cost. A significant part of us wants to control, dominate, certainly not give our very selves away. This brings us to the point where once again we have to choose: to control or love. As we are brought to this choice, which we think should be so easy and in fact find so hard, we discover that God's gentle love has prepared us for it. Usually there is no one movement of decision. It is strung out over a series of days and weeks and even years as the truth about us becomes clear, as God touches us in the silence, as the events of our lives keep bringing us back to this central drama; and we choose.

This process of stripping us of our wilfulness continues, for while we have given over the control of our lives in ways deeper than ever before, there remain parts of our personalities that still have not surfaced, that have not yet been drawn into this central direction of our lives. Once again the events of our lives conspire to take away anything we might cling to and lead us into yet another moment of choice. We have come to the point where we really want to follow in Jesus' way of living on the will of the Father. We do this by trying to discern his will in all things. When we come to a decision, therefore, we try to discern what is his will, and make it our own. It is this very process that becomes the threshing floor of our hearts. We make a good decision, faithful to our commitment to follow Jesus in all things; we get accustomed to it; and then circumstances beyond our control so alter the situation that the decision has to be gone through again. This happens time after time. We struggle with God's will; give ourselves over to it; and the other side of that surrender have an experience of insight and serenity that frees us to go out to others with new vitality and simplicity. Then the situation is changed and we are once again thrown back into discernment.

As this becomes a distinct pattern in our lives we come to recognize that something of great importance is taking place and that the revelation of what God is doing here will come as a gift in the deep silence of prayer, not in talking it over, or thinking it through on our own, though both of those have their place. Eventually the silence discloses its secret. Each time things get changed around, we come to accept this as God's will. When this happens consolation follows. If we fight it there is desolation. What the silence reveals to us is that in all of this switching our willfulness, our need to have our will predominate, is being broken. As it is broken, we are freed to trust, to accept the gift that is really being given. This is what we have been resisting. Now we see it and let go.

Other things come together to extend this stripping into all aspects of our lives. For example, it can happen that those we love are taken away; it can be the simple question of relocation in one's job, the entering of a religious community or any of a series of common everyday occurrences. No matter the cause, the end result is the same. A situation is created where one has to learn to love when there is little or no feedback. We must love; but without regard for the fruits of that action; or, in faith, we must hand those fruits over to God. In other situations the friend is still there, but something begins to happen to our interior world. The keen attachment, the need to hold on to the other slowly fades. Is this a deeper, purer love than the love of attachment, or does this only reveal what has been true all along, namely that we never loved in the first place? The very facing of this possibility is a purgation in itself.[39] In either case, we see that something happens to us; and each sets up a choice. Do I

13

learn to love in a way that is less selfish and deeper? Do I choose to be faithful, to do what is good for the other, even when the fruits of that do not seem to come back to me?

Parallel to this is what happens to us as we are brought face to face with our own limits to give to those we love. This can be a question of facing one aspect of our ingrained selfishness; or it can be a confrontation with our finitude; or it can be that the circumstances of our lives just make it impossible to be with those we love when they are in need. However it happens, interior and exterior events bring us to the point where we can do little or nothing for those we love. Or, having done what we could, we see that it is not enough. This throws us back on ourselves; and we discover how truly poor we are.

Once again we have to choose. Do we get angry or fearful? Do we still want to control? Or can we recognize that we are only being forced to see what was always true anyway—that we have to rely on God alone? The rest is all illusion. Can we learn to love when that love seems to be useless, when seemingly we cannot help those we love? All there is is the very being in love itself. Can we pour out our hearts trusting that he will take care of those we love? This seems to be exactly parallel to what has happened to our prayer. We have to learn to be seemingly useless, letting God act in a way that transcends our experience and understanding. There is no use pretending; this is killing.

In all of these things there emerges a pattern. Something happens to us, something is taken away, and we have to choose to deal with this in faith. As this effects the different areas of our lives, our loves, our work, our sense of ourselves, and so on, they are all gradually drawn into the fundamental attitude that is unifying and transforming our previously scattered selves and lives. We are learning to trust in God, to place our lives in his hands and to follow where he leads us whether we can understand or experience it as trust or not. When something happens to us now that causes us confusion or suffering we no longer react, 'Why did this happen to me?' or, 'How do I get out of this?' Rather we find ourselves asking, 'What is God trying to teach me here?'[40]

This increasing trust in God changes entirely how we understand ourselves and what happens to us. It frees us to respond to the Lord in a new way. Here the passive night of sense and the active night of spirit constantly flow into each other effecting a huge integration and simplification of the entire personality. Still, it is only as we look back on this whole process that we can see that this terrible stripping was the gift of a gentle Father, a gift that was right on the mark for it touched us exactly where we needed to be changed.

Some Fruits of Gentleness

What does this growing integration look like? There is a greater resilience and generosity in one's everyday life, a greater ability to commit one's self and follow through. There is a growing freedom to cope with the real problems. For example, we begin to see that in the past we often did what we needed to do and called it our apostolate. Now we try to find out what people need and learn how we can help them. This is not necessarily very exciting. It tends to be routine; but it is important: teaching these children to spell, trying to support people whose marriages are strained, listening to young men who might like to become good priests. Whatever it is, we do it with a simple dedication and a renewed freedom. Indeed, this is true to such an extent that we can say, 'If I should die tomorrow I would be glad to have spent my life doing this'.

There is no hidden agenda. When we sit down to pray, more and more we are drawn into this vague, bland quiet. There are no pretences. It is not exciting. We don't understand much of what is happening; but our hearts are there. Mass is a similar affair. It is so everyday, so plain. We don't feel like an alleluia from head to toe; we hardly feel anything; but we are always there. We are simply saying our prayers. Yet, while prayer is becoming more vague, the concern for being faithful grows ever stronger.[41] For example, if we are away for a few days and it is hard to find a time and place to pray, without giving it much thought, we find ourselves looking forward to getting home and spending more time in prayer. Of course, when we get back it is elusive again; and we hardly notice how really concerned about it we have become. Instead we tend to worry that we really aren't as serious as we ought to be; and all we can do is keep

15

going back each day to the silence where it often seems that nothing is happening. Still, when we talk this over with our spiritual director we have to admit to ourselves that we really are waiting for God, and with God, even if it is in a way we do not understand.

When we are working there is the same stripping down to essentials. We are just teaching, or taking care of the kids, or visiting the sick. Our friendships show the same simplicity and directness. We are deeply loyal; and the possessiveness slips away. We speak to people directly and invite a direct, honest response. We also begin to find that our hearts are open to embrace the agony of those around us. The defences we have built to protect us have been stripped away; and it is only God's love pouring into our hearts that sustains us, that sends us out to others in compassion.

While the people we are describing are becoming free to be more active and resolute in their exterior lives, they are becoming increasingly passive in prayer. More and more they sense how dependent they are on the Father; and they accept this, are even thankful for it. Indeed, they long to be possessed by the Father even more. Further, in this growing integration, this unification of the person, there is a coming to know the self as we really are—before God, and before God we see that we are weak, fragile, wayward, self-centered. In short, we are sinners.[42] This becomes obvious. We probably commit few sins now; but we are terribly aware of ourselves as sinners, as people who are cherished by God and who just don't respond adequately to this gift. This is a new realization, something we have never seen before because we could never bear to admit it. Now the love of God flooding into our hearts in the bland quiet of contemplation frees us to face it, and strengthens us to endure the pain of seeing it.

This sense of sin is not the same as depression or lack of self-confidence or guilt. As a matter of fact, it is exactly the opposite. Up to this time there has always been lurking in us the terrible suspicion that really we are all alone in the universe, and that no one and no thing can save us from this annihilating isolation. This dark inflow of God, that we do not understand, begins to heal our hearts of this primordial terror.[43] Further, even when we could believe there was a loving God, we have been haunted by the feeling that he could not love us. Somehow we were unlovable, radically unacceptable. We could pretend, trying desperately to do all the right things, but God always knew. Now he comes pouring into our hearts in a way that slips under our understanding as well as our defences and fears; and he subverts our suspicious, guilty hearts. He is healing us. We look at the Crucified One and just know that we are not alone, that we are loved.

The result of all this is that you have a healed human heart.[44] You have men and women who have a gift for friendship, and a good self image. They know they are loved and can love in return.[45] They move easily in different situations. They know their abilities and are decent and hard-working. Their lives are usually stable, if a bit bland. They do not seek God as a substitute for human love. They love him for his own sake, though they may not be aware of it. They are very faithful to all their commitments; but they are aware of different levels of motivation in themselves and others. They live with a healthy scepticism of their own motives. They say their prayers; go to Mass; and are deeply concerned about fidelity. Usually they can not see the growing fidelity and longing for God that is moving in their depths. But occasionally, there are moments, on retreat or at crucial turning points in their lives, or just out of the blue, when what lies hidden and growing in their depths moves to the surface and they are nearly overwhelmed by their longing for God.[46]

Even with all of this, they know it is not enough. They know they are worthwhile, successful human beings, and that that just is not enough. As they stand before the Father in the darkness of contemplation, it seems to be nothing. Still, the Father loves them, and this keeps them going; as a matter of fact it gives them a deep peace. They are his little ones; and Jesus' word, 'I give you peace, a peace the world cannot give', takes on a new meaning.[47]

As they start to look at themselves from within this peace, they start to notice that many of the imperfections that used to afflict them have dropped away. They are much freer, more simple than they used to be. They are not so angry; are less concerned about praise. They are much more tolerant and compassionate. They are free to do their work, say their prayers and trust in God. The illusions of achieving immortality through their integrity or moral perfection, or even their progress in prayer, have been given up. Only God can save them; and they are accepting of this. They are loyal and full of real hope, no longer the enthusiasts who could so easily be discouraged. The relentless gentleness of God, working through this mingling of the passive night of sense and the active night of spirit has integrated and simplified them. They are much more gentle than they ever were before.

If we think for a moment of people like Mother Teresa, Dorothy Day, Dom Helder Camera or Bede Griffiths, this same gentleness comes through. To meet them is to see someone transparently simple, gentle to the core; and from that core reaching out to others in universal compassion. They have no pretensions about their own way to this gentleness and speak about it in very simple terms: fidelity, prayer, joining themselves to Christ in the agony of others. They speak of the same realities of which John speaks. And when we see them we know that this is what it is to be really human. To meet them is to be confronted with what we are all called to be. Through their lives and words we hear once again the invitation of Jesus:[48] *Come to me, all who labour and are heavy laden, and I will give you rest. Take my yoke upon you, and learn from me; for I am gentle and lowly of heart, and you will find rest for your souls. For my yoke is easy, and my burden is light.*

NOTES

1. Crisogono de Jesus OCD, *The Life of St John of the Cross*, trans. Kathleen Pond. New York, Harper & Brothers, and London, Longmans, Green and Co Ltd, 1958, p. 75. The author cites the manuscript evidence for this quotation.
2. Ibid., pp. 194-5.   3. Ibid., pp. 196-7.
4. Ibid., p. 200.   5. Cf. *Living Flame* II, 17.
6. *Ascent* I, 13, 3-4.   7. Cf. *Living Flame* II, 34.
8. Cf. *Ascent* I, 15, 1. This is a linchpin of John's whole thought. As men and women move towards God they gradually learn to trust in him, not themselves; and so are free of the arrogance of trying to save themselves, the real horror of original sin.
9. This, for example, is quite different from Mark's picture of Jesus on the cross. For a redactional study of the different passion narratives with a special emphasis on Jesus' prayer, see David M. Stanley SJ, *Jesus in Gethsemane*. New York, Paulist Press, 1980. It is interesting to note that these were also the last words of John of the Cross.
10. I am assuming that *Ascent-Night* is essentially a single work. See E.W. Trueman Dicken, *The Crucible of Love*. New York, Sheed and Ward, and London, Darton, Longman and Todd Ltd., 1963, pp. 215-37.
11. *Living Flame* II, 16-19.   12. *Living Flame* IV, 5.
13. There are places where John leaves aside the logical order to make sure he covers something he considers of importance, e.g. in *Ascent* III he twice leaves his main topic, the active night of spirit, to deal with material pertaining to the active night of sense. He does this in Chapters 18-26 and 35-44.
14. Cf. *Dark Night* I, 1, 1 and 8, 1 where he clearly states that the passive night of sense is proper to beginners, whereas the active night of spirit is characteristic of proficients, cf. *Ascent* II, 15, 1 and 5. The passive night of sense precedes and sets up the active night of spirit, but then both continue simultaneously.
15. *Ascent* I, Chapters 6-10 where he takes each of these in turn, and illustrates his point.
16. *Ascent* I, 13, 4.
17. *Ascent* I, 14, 2. It is this fire of love that draws us to Christ and fills our hearts with a 'sensible' experience of his presence. This fire will break forth in the *Living Flame* as the Spirit; but now its true depth is only vaguely sensed. Now it begins to unite us to Jesus and provides us with the motivation needed to enter and sustain the active night of sense.

18. For the absolute necessity of this, see *Dark Night* I, 3, 3.
19. *Dark Night* I, 8, 3, 'they cannot advance a step in meditation, as they used to, now that the interior sensory faculties are engulfed in this night.'
20. Twice John gives us rules for discerning this crucial passage so that we will enter it at God's invitation and only at his invitation. Cf. *Dark Night* I, 9 and 10; *Ascent* II, 13-15.
21. Cf. for example, *Ascent* II, 7, 3-12.
22. Among other places, see *Living Flame* I, 23-24.
23. Cf. in particular annotations Nos. 2, 15 and 18. Fr Fleming's commentary makes this abundantly clear. See his *A Contemporary Reading of the Spiritual Exercises*, Institute of Jesuit Sources, St. Louis, Missouri, 1976, pp. 6-9.
24. *Ascent* I, 14, 2.   25. *Dark Night* I, 11, 1 and 2.
26. *Dark Night* II, 11, 2.   27. *Living Flame* I, 3.
28. Cf. *Dark Night* I, 2, 1.   29. Cf. *Dark Night* I, 2, 4.
30. Cf. *Dark Night* I, 3, 1 and 5, 1.   31. Cf. *Dark Night* I, 2, 3.
32. Cf. *Dark Night* I, 5, 3.   33. Cf. *Dark Night* I, 4, 7.
34. Cf. *Dark Night* I, 5, 2.
35. Cf. Trueman Dicken, op. cit., pp. 249-54.
36. Cf. Isaiah 30:15-21.   37. Cf. Psalm 95.
38. John 1:38.
39. T.S. Eliot sums this up exactly in the line 'The unattached devotion which might pass for devotionless'. It 'might pass' for that; but it isn't. See 'The Dry Salvages', line 63, in *Four Quartets*, New York: Harcourt, Brace and World, 1971, p. 38.
40. Cf. *Living Flame* II, 30 and III, 29; also Trueman Dicken, op. cit., pp. 261-62 on the voiding of memory.
41. Cf. *Dark Night* I, 9, 3, the second of John's three signs; but especially *Dark Night* I, 11, 2.
42. Cf. *Dark Night* I, 12, 2.
43. I use a progressive expression because this is an ongoing process; and the very roots of fear and guilt will only be eradicated in the passive night of spirit. Cf. *Dark Night* II, 2 and 3.
44. In the *Dark Night* I, 12, 7 he starts going through the imperfections he dealt with in Chapters 2-7 and shows how they are healed. This is also the main subject of Chapter 13.
45. Cf. *Dark Night* I, 12, 8.   46. *Dark Night* I, 11, 1-4.
47. John 14:27.
48. Matthew 11:28-30; see John Meier's useful comments on this text in his *Matthew*, Wilmington, Del.: Michael Glazier, 1980, pp. 125-28.

SELECT BIBLIOGRAPHY

St John of the Cross in English

St John of the Cross, *Complete Works*, trans. Allison Peers, Anthony Clarke, 1974.

The Collected Works of St John of the Cross, trans. Kieran Kavanaugh OCD and Otilio Rodriguez OCD, with Introductions by Kieran Kavanaugh OCD, Nelson 1966.

St John of the Cross, *The Ascent of Mount Carmel* and *The Dark Night*, Simplified Version, John Venard OCD, Published by The Order of Discalced Carmelites, Anglo-Irish Province, 1981.

Poems of St John of the Cross, trans. Roy Campbell, Harvill Press, 1951.

Lamps of Fire, Daily Readings with St John of the Cross, edited by Elizabeth Ruth ODC, Darton, Longman & Todd, 1985.

John of the Cross: Selected Writings, ed. with Introduction by Kieran Kavanaugh OCD, Classics of Western Spirituality, SPCK, 1987.

PILGRIMAGE AND POSSESSION, Conversion in the Writings of St John of the Cross and St Teresa by Sister Eileen Mary SLG. SLG Press 1983 (Fairacres Publication 86). Price £1.25.

Sister Eileen Mary begins this study by disputing the assumption that the writings of St John of the Cross are fiercely world- and life-denying: he does challenge us by asking, 'How much do you want God? How much do you want to live from your true self?', but if we respond with strong desire and good courage, the life-long way of conversion to which he points us will not destroy our humanity, it will reveal and enlarge it. *The Ascent of Mount Carmel* and *The Dark Night of the Soul* are seen to describe what is likely to happen when we invite and allow God to take the initiative in our life and prayer.

Aware that St John and St Teresa inhabited a thought-world different from our own, Sister Eileen Mary insists that no merely cultural or social factors can affect our fundamental human condition as pilgrims, however that condition may be interpreted. For her this has been strikingly demonstrated by the correspondence she sees between the pattern which emerges in St Teresa's *Interior Castle* and the ancient Chinese philosophy of *I-Ching*.

CARMELITE ASCENT, An Introduction to St Teresa and St John of the Cross by Mother Mary Clare SLG. SLG Press 1973 (Fairacres Publication 33). Price £1.25.

This introduction to the spirituality of the leaders of the Carmelite Reform offers brief descriptions of the historical and biographical background of their writings together with suggestions for beginning the study of their works.

A COMPLETE LIST OF FAIRACRES PUBLICATIONS IS AVAILABLE ON REQUEST FROM:

SLG Press
Fairacres, Oxford OX4 1TB, England